C000056161

IMAGES OF WALES

WHITCHURCH
AND LLANDAFF NORTH

IMAGES OF WALES

WHITCHURCH
AND LLANDAFF NORTH

STEVE NICHOLAS

TEMPUS

*I would like to dedicate this book to my cousin
Gareth Newing of Whitchurch. He was sadly
taken away from us at the young age of eighteen.
He will be remembered with much love and
affection by all his family and friends.*

Frontispiece: Melingriffith Tinplate Works

First published 2005

Tempus Publishing Limited
The Mill, Brimscombe Port,
Stroud, Gloucestershire, GL5 2QG
www.tempus-publishing.com

© Steve Nicholas, 2005

The right of Steve Nicholas to be identified as the Author
of this work has been asserted in accordance with the
Copyrights, Designs and Patents Act 1988.

All rights reserved. No part of this book may be reprinted
or reproduced or utilised in any form or by any electronic,
mechanical or other means, now known or hereafter invented,
including photocopying and recording, or in any information
storage or retrieval system, without the permission in writing
from the Publishers.

British Library Cataloguing in Publication Data.
A catalogue record for this book is available from the British Library.

ISBN 0 7524 3635 X

Typesetting and origination by Tempus Publishing Limited.
Printed in Great Britain.

Contents

Acknowledgements

It has only been possible to produce this volume through the generous contributions of photographs, information and help from so many people. Many of them are thanked in the list below. Apologies to any that I have inadvertently left out.

Geoff Atkins, Tony Atkins, W.G. Atkins, Tony Baird, Haydn Bartley, Bev Beynon, John and Pauline Blakemore, Olwen Booker, Ceri Bowden, Gwyn Bowden, Graham Clements, Tom Collard, Maureen Collett, Bob Coombes, Reg Cox, Alan and Ann Davies, Mair Davies, Kelvin Dean, Phil Edwards, Mike Eklund, Mike Evans, Trevor Evans, Des Farnham, Haydn Farnham, Alison Fear, Nick Howard and all at the Radyr and Morganstown (Melingriffith) Band website, Tal Gardiner, Lyn George, Peter George, Les Gibbon, Keith Gregory, Gordon Hann, Ted Hayman, Michael Howe, Roger Jones, Stan Jones, Tudor Jones, Terry Kidner, Jan King, Robin Lasbury, Hywell Lewis, Mair Llewellynn, Alan Lyons, Derek Matthews, Alan Mitchell, Bernard Mitchell, Ernie Mitchell, George Morris, David Nicholas Snr, Phil Parker, Dai Parsons, Graham Paton, Sally Paton, David Paul, Pam Phillips, David Phillips, George Randall, Frank Rees, Willy Rees, Gwyn Rhys, Pat Roberts, Bryn Rossiter, Des Rowley, Dai Rowley, Jeff Rowley, Suzanne Rowley, Tony Rowley, Trenuth Seager, Gareth Simmonds, Ian Stokes, Carl Stickler, Jim Taverner, A. and G. Taylor, Ivor Tout, Ray Tout, Anthony Trigg, Jean Watson (*née* Blakemore), Alan Welfoot, Angie Williams, Chris Williams, Pat Yorath, the Galpin family.

Introduction

During the early months of 2003 I wanted to have a go at building a website. I decided to construct a community website which would encourage visitors to share photographs of the area from their personal collections.

I was surprised how quickly and popular the website became, and I never thought for a minute that I would be receiving e-mails from places such as Montreal, Florida, Hong Kong, Washington, Perth, etc. I realised that my website will not be around forever so through this book I wanted to produce more of a permanent record. The reason I have included Whitchurch and Llandaff North in one book is because up until 1902 Llandaff North formed part of the Whitchurch parish. Evidence of this can be seen today on the walls of Hawthorn Road Junior School in Llandaff North, the school originally opened as the Whitchurch Board School.

Whitchurch and Llandaff North has a fascinating history, however, because of the nature of this book it has not been possible to cover the history of the area much before the twentieth century. There have however been several publications which look at the history of the area in much more detail and these are available at local libraries.

Old photographs revive our memories and give us an idea of how our ancestors worked, played and built up the community that we live in today. Many of the photographs in this book will re-awaken the memories of the older generation while at the same time show the younger generation a glimpse of the past. The latter part of the twentieth century has seen the most change with the demise of the Melingriffith Tinplate Works, Radyr Railway Yard, the Glamorgan Canal and numerous local farms. Many of the images in this book are from old postcards but many are also from personal collections, sent to me via my website. I have tried to use as many older photographs as possible to illustrate how the area has changed over the years but I have also included photographs up until the end of the twentieth century, with time these too will become old photographs!

As with any work of this kind there are bound to be minor slips, errors and spelling mistakes. I have made every effort to provide as much accurate information as possible. Some readers may be able to add or make corrections to some of the information contained within. I would be very glad to receive either corrections or further information in case these can be incorporated in a revised edition.

I hope that this collection of images will provide you with a window to the past and give you much enjoyment.

Steve Nicholas
May 2005

one

Out and About

Whitchurch village, *c*. 1900. The thatched shop in this view is J.A. Lewis the drapers, in the 1980s it was Percy Thomas Florists Ltd and is presently an Italian restaurant.

Postcard view of Llandaff Station and the Hill, Llandaff North, *c*. 1900.

St Mary's church on Old Church Road, *c*. 1900. The site was converted into a memorial garden in 1974.

ST. MARY'S GARDENS
THIS DISUSED CHURCHYARD IS THE SITE
OF ST. MARY'S CHURCH BUILT IN THE 17TH
CENTURY INCORPORATING THE PORCH
OF A CHAPEL BUILT HERE IN THE 15TH
CENTURY. THE CHURCH WAS DEMOLISHED
IN 1904 AFTER BEING REPLACED BY A NEW
ST. MARY'S CHURCH BUILT AT CHURCH
ROAD IN 1883-84.

THE GARDENS WERE CONSTRUCTED BY
CARDIFF CITY COUNCIL AND OFFICIALLY
OPENED BY COUNCILLOR H. E. DAVIES.
O.B.E. M.A. ON 7TH APRIL. 1974.

St Mary's church wall plaque commemorating the opening of the memorial garden in 1974.

All Saints church, Llandaff North, *c.* 1900.

Postcard view of the Cow and Snuffers at Llandaff Yard, *c.* 1900.

Right: Carved in stone above the window of the Cow and Snuffers is the head of Benjamin Disraeli who became Prime Minister of Great Britain in 1868 and for a second time in 1874. It is believed that Disraeli visited the Cow and Snuffers in around 1838 while he was courting Mary Lewis of Greenmeadow mansion, Tongwynlais.

Below: The Glamorganshire Canal and lock near the Cow and Snuffers at Llandaff Yard, *c.* 1900.

Canal Lock & "Cow & Snuffers" Llandaff Yard, Glam. No. 132.

The site of the Old Turnpike on the junction of Llantrisant Road and Bridge Road, *c.* 1900.

Tyn Y Parc Road, *c.* 1910. The brook seen in this photograph is known as Nant Waedlyd, the last native Welsh Prince of Morgannwg (Glamorgan), Iestyn ap Gwrgant, was killed in a battle north of Rhiwbina. It is said that so much blood was shed at the battle that the brook became known as the 'Bloody Brook'.

Pantmawr Road, *c.* 1910. This section is between the Hollybush pub and Northern Avenue.

Bishops Road, *c.* 1910. The three-storey building on the left belonged to Whitchurch farmer Tom Samuel, it contained a gas engine which cut chaff and sliced mangolds. The chaff was bundled into bales and lowered from the top floor using a lift. The centre building is the fire station and Whitchurch parish council office, the first floor was the council chamber and the fire station was below.

Whitchurch Mental Hospital, *c.* 1910. Opened in 1906 the hospital originally housed over 700 patients. During the First World War the hospital was designated a military war hospital under the command of Lieutenant Colonel Edwin Goodall. To this day patients with psychiatric problems are still being cared for at the hospital.

A view of Llandaff Bridge looking east, *c.* 1920. The bridge at Llandaff has been in this area for over 230 years. The bridge was also a great viewing point for spectators of the regattas held at Llandaff Rowing Club. The rowing club has been sited on the River Taff since 1879.

Kelston Road, Whitchurch, *c.* 1920.

Whitchurch post office, *c.* 1930. It is presently Darlows Estate Agents.

The Glamorgan Canal near the Melingriffith Tinplate Works, *c.* 1920. Lock Cottage is on the left, Oak Cottage is on the right and was for many years the home of the Williams family.

A recent photograph of Oak Cottage taken in 2004. The building has hardly changed since being built well over 100 years ago, some parts of the building are said to date back to the sixteenth century. Until recently it was owned and occupied by Griffith Williams. In the doorway stands Frank Rees, a good friend of Griff's.

The *Emerald Isle*, 1930. This engine was used at the Melingriffith Tinplate Works. The driver is Oliver Collard and the latcher is Mr Tilly.

The *Emerald Isle*, *c*. 1950. Stan Jones of Heol Booker is at the footplate and the driver is Peter Ireson.

Hailey Park bowling green, *c.* 1940. The brick works chimney stack can be seen in the background towards the left of the picture.

Foreland Road, Whitchurch, *c.* 1950.

Galpin's electrical appliance shop on Merthyr Road decorated for the Coronation of Queen Elizabeth II in 1953.

Manor Way looking north to the railway bridge at Pen y Dre, *c.* 1950.

The entrance to the Melingriffith Tinplate Works at Whitchurch in 1958.

The man who died of a broken heart

THIS is the story of Bert King, of Cardiff—the man who died of a broken heart.

Bert had one interest in life—the Melingriffith Tinplate Works at Taff's Well.

He was born there. He worked there for 40 years and rose to become works manager.

But the works will soon die. And Bert has died, too.

A hard blow

The news that the Melingriffith was to go struck Mr. King, of St. Angela Road, Heath, Cardiff, a hard blow.

But cheery, soft-spoken Bert watched the workers start to dismantle the machinery without complaining.

Only when he got home at night did he tell his wife, Freda, how
much the place meant to him,
how unhapppy he was to see it
doomed. . . .

On Wednesday, he paid his usual visit to his daughter, Mrs. Joan Platt, at her Court Road, Cardiff, home. He sat down, passed a word on the weather . . . and never spoke again.

When Mrs. Platt touched him, she found her father was dead.

The last days

Doing her best to suppress her sobbing, Mrs. Platt told last night of her father's last days.

"He was dreadfully upset that the works at Taffs Well were closing down," she said.

"He was born there, you know. His grandfather was caretaker
in a cottage on the grounds which is now the gatekeeper's lodge.

"And the old place meant every-
thing to him. He was heart-
broken at the closure news."

Yesterday a post mortem was held to determine the cause of Mr. King's death. The findings will be announced.

Last night, Mr. Emrys Pride, Cardiff consulting engineer who was a fellow member with Mr. King on the city Productivity Committee, said:

"Mr. King was a genial, hard-working man. Always ready wih a happy word—and always with a good scheme to overcome one of the committee's difficulties.

A newspaper article from 15 November 1957 about Bert King, who worked at the Melingriffith Tinplate Works for forty years and passed away following its closure.

Whitchurch railway station, 28 May 1957.

The Melingriffith water pump was built
in 1807 to pump water from the work's
tail race into the canal below Melingriffith
lock. When the canal was finally shut,
the pump was abandoned and the
canal filled in. Although a listed ancient
monument, the structure was on the point
of collapse until its restoration in 1974.
Many thousands of pounds were spent
on restoring the pump and constructing
a new watercourse when the original
feeder disappeared under the new housing
development on the site of the works.

The construction of the new road bridge on Manor Way (A470) over the Coryton railway line near Whitchurch railway station in 1958.

Opposite above: Coryton Halt, Whitchurch, June 1958.

Opposite below: Christchurch, Hazelhurst Road, *c.* 1960. Dwindling attendances and the large costs of running and maintaining it meant the church was no longer viable. They moved into the Sunday school rooms opposite which are still used today. The church was demolished in around 1976 and flats were built on the land by local builders Newbarry.

Rival gangs fight it out at station

Above: Llandaff North station, *c.* 1960. No. 5600 was built at Swindon in 1924. Over 200 engines of this type were built and were mainly used for hauling coal from the pit-head to the docks. The destination of the diesel carriage train in this photograph was Barry Island.

Left: A newspaper article reports a fight between two rival gangs at Llandaff North station, *c.* 1960.

BOOTS and fists flew late last night as rival gangs met on a railway footbridge at Llandaff North Station, Cardiff. One gang, said to be from Taffs Well, caught the 11.5 train to Cardiff and arrived at Llandaff where another crowd of youths from the Western Avenue Estate were waiting for them.

As the train pulled in, the Cardiff gang raced on to the footbridge shouting insults at young men on the train.

Women passenges stayed in the train as battle broke out on the platform and on the bridge. All the men—about 20 altogether—were between the ages of 18 and 25.

As the battle became more violent, railway police and local police were called.

Black eyes

It is believed that the men from Taffs Well were looking for two men from Caldy Road, Cardiff, and had come to "sort them out." The local youths heard of their intention and prepared a reception party for them.

Several men were later treated for black eyes, cut lips and damaged ribs, but no serious injuries were sustained.

The incident is the worst of its kind so far along the valley line which is often the scene of hooliganism—especially at weekends.

The names of two men were taken by the railway police.

GWR 5700 Class No. 3681 travelling north through Radyr station in May 1963. The Melingriffith Tinplate Works can be seen in the background.

Ray Tout on-board GWR engine 7205, at Radyr Yard, *c.* 1965.

Forest Farm, *c.* 1970. This area has changed considerably over the last thirty years with the construction of Forest Farm industrial estate. Some businesses on the estate include Walmart Asda superstore, G.E. Healthcare, A.B. Electronics, Batleys and British Telecom.

People queue for bread at the Honey Pot bakers on Penlline Road, *c.* 1983. Due to heavy snowfall people were unable to drive to the supermarkets to do their shopping.

Whitchurch Common during a snowstorm, *c.* 1983.

THIS AVENUE OF TREES
WAS PLANTED ON BEHALF OF
THE 2ND EVACUATION UNIT
OF THE
UNITED STATES ARMY
AS A TOKEN OF GRATITUDE
FOR THE HOSPITALITY EXTENDED TO THEM
BY THE PARISHIONERS OF WHITCHURCH
DURING THE SECOND WORLD WAR
1939 - 1945

Plaque commemorating the planting of trees on Whitchurch Common on behalf of the 2nd Evacuation Unit of the United States Army during the Second World War. In 1944 the unit set up a large tented camp on Whitchurch Common.

A British Rail Standard 4 Class No. 80080 on the 150th anniversary of the Taff Vale Railway passing Llandaff Loop Junction signal box. The signal box opened in 1900 and closed in 1998. The box pictured here replaced an earlier signal box known as Llandaff Fourth Line Junction signal box.

Atlas Express parcel carrier's depot, c. 1983. Located on Ty Mawr Road, they were originally based in Leckwith, Cardiff, and moved to the Whitchurch site in the early 1960s.

Atlas Express, *c.* 1985. The buildings were owned by W.J. Thomas furniture removals. Atlas closed down their Whitchurch depot in August 1985.

An Atlas Express lorry attempts to leave the yard but is clearly having difficulty due to the snow, *c.* 1983.

The Crown pub as it was in 2003. Built sometime before 1878, it was demolished in March 2005.

Whitchurch police station, Bishops Road. Built in 1908, it was demolished in 2003 and is soon to be replaced by luxury apartments.

two

Schooldays

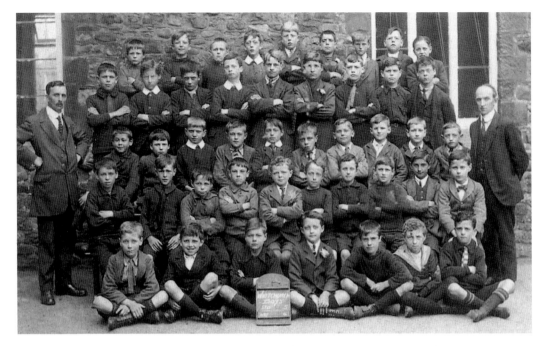

Eglwys Newydd Boys' School, standard 5, *c.* 1918. Ivor Vaughan Yorath is in the front row fourth from the left. Mr Sam Jones, the school headmaster, is standing on the left.

Watson Road School, 1928. Iris Cox is sixth from the right in the front row. Second from the right is Reg Cox.

Eglwys Newydd Boys' School, April 1928. Thomas Collett is third from the left in the front row.

Watson Road School, c. 1930. Iris Cox is third from the left in the second row from the front.

Glan Y Nant Infants' School, 1931. Johnny Yorath is standing in the front row, sixth from the left.

Hawthorn Road Infants' School, *c.* 1935. In the front row Billy Lee is second from the left, Ray Tout is fourth, Jimmy Edwards is sixth and John Ball is seventh. In the second row Sylvia Thorne is second from the left, ? Whitcombe is third and Peter Whitcombe is ninth. In the third row Mervyn Francis is third from the left, Fred Burrows is fourth and Derek Smith is fifth.

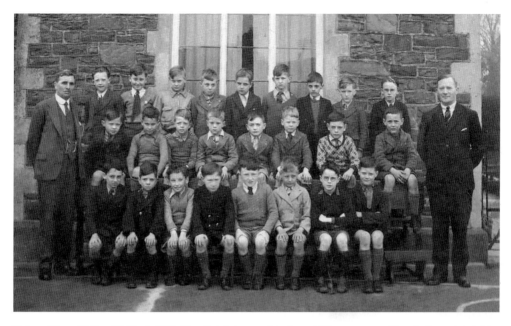

Eglwys Newydd Boys' School, 1936. Don Leigh is seated in the middle row, second boy in from the right.

Hawthorn Road Junior School, *c.* 1938. Gloria Watkins is standing in the back row, second from the left.

Hawthorn Junior School, St David's Day, 1939. Gwyn Rhys is second from the left, and John Rhys is third from the left.

Whitchurch Secondary School, 1943/44. In the middle row Eric Lewis is fourth from the left and Tudor Jones is eighth. In the front row Brynmor Williams is first on the left and Tudor Lloyd is seventh.

Hawthorn Road Junior School, 1947. In the back row Gerald Purdon is fifth from the left and Raymond Knight is seventh. In the middle row Betty Troake is second from the left and Jean Whittle is fourth. In the front row Jean Blakemore is second from the left, Rosalie Jones is fourth and Ann Lansdowne is ninth.

Hawthorn Road Junior School, c. 1950. In the back row John Barry is fifth from the left, Billy Lee sixth from the left, and Derek Smith is tenth. In the middle row Jimmy Edwards is tenth from the left. From left to right, front row: Donald Hann, Gordon Thorn, Mervyn Francis, -?-, Ray Tout, John Bounds.

Hawthorn Road Junior School, *c.* 1951. Ian Stokes is first on the left.

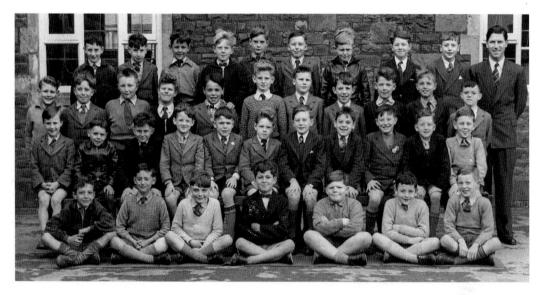

Eglwys Newydd Boys' School, *c.* 1954. From left to right, back row: Michael Flanagan, Eric Priday, Peter Wayne Jones, –?–, Ralph Larner, Alan Biss, Michael Martin, Malcolm Wyatt, Ralph ?, Mr Evans. Third row: Brynley Rossiter, Alan Pasley, Geoffrey Richards, Robert Owen, John Bevan, Richard Salmon, –?–, Martin Evans, Derek Matthews, John Joshua, Martin Howells. Second row: Michael Jones, –?–, ? Kemp, Richard Edwards, Phillip Gerrard, Peter Smith, Gordon Donn, John Marsh, –?–, David Davies, Peter Dow. Front row: John Perry, David Stephens, Peter Haylock, John Hyatt, Richard Alun John, Phillip Boswell, Alan Spear.

Eglwys Newydd Boys' School, class 5A, 1955. From left to right, back row: -?-, Raymond Durnell, Russell Davies, -?-, Alan Welfoot, Donald Norman, -?-, -?-, Alan Hogg. Third row: Mr Lewis Conybeare, Raymond Singleton, Ivor Gerrish, Greg Rogers, -?-, Terry Holland, David Lewis, Geoffrey Upsdell, Roy Priday, Robert Bennett. Second row (seated): Graham Usher, -?-, Ceri Lewis, -?-, -?-, Michael Wedlake, -?-, -?-, -?-, -?-. Front row: Melvyn(?) Herbert, Phillip Stilliard, -?-, -?-, Ricky Freer-Huish.

Eglwys Newydd Boys' School, class 5B, 1955. From left to right, front row: Jeff Reese, -?-. Second row: Dai Light, Alan Williams, ? Phillips, ? Phillips, Graham Bowsher, Ian Loma, Stephen Rees, Eddy Rees, Leighton Thomas, -?-, Georgy Jones. Third row: Glyn Fitzgerald, ? Terret, Ted Terret, Michael Griffiths, Michael King, -?-, -?-, Austin Roberts, Malcolm Griffiths. Back row: Mr Sunderland, Robert Short, -?-, Stuart Alney, Glyn Brown, Lawrence Dyer, Kenny Lee, Robert Spurway, Graham Robbins, John Onley.

Mr Thomas (left), headmaster of Eglwys
Newydd Boys' School, and schoolteacher
Mr James, *c.* 1955.

Eglwys Newydd teacher Mr Lewis
Conybeare on a school trip to the Elan
Valley, *c.* 1940.

Eglwys Newydd Boys' School, c. 1956. From left to right, back row: Mr Denzil Morgan, Christopher ?, David Richards, Alan Stevens, Patrick Webber, Gordon Canning, Colin Davies, Eric James, Malcolm Piper, Tony Rowley, -?-, Mike Hargest. Middle row: Gerald Thompson, Alun Bladden, Colin Lynch, Michael Wills, ? Harfoot, Geoff Herbert, Roger Marriott, John Boyce, Martin Lewis. Front row: Bobby Pullin, Gordon Oliver, Peter Ashley, Alan Taylor, Malcolm Jones, Graham Stokes, Gerald Wright, Paul Tracy, Gary Farnell, Gordon Jennings.

Hawthorn Road Junior School, 1955. Cardiff City Golden Jubilee. Linda Paul is in the front row, first from the right.

Whitchurch Grammar School under 16's cricket team, 1956. Mike Evans is in the back row, second from the left, and John Hitchen is in the front row, fifth from the left.

Eglwys Newydd Boys' School, c. 1957. From left to right, back row: Clive Meacham, Gwyn Bowden, Jonathan Davies, Richard Salmon. Third row: Ralph Larner, Geoffrey Richards, Robert Watson, Peter Haylock, Robert Sherlock, John Joshua, John Perry, Guy Jennings, Jonathan Phillips, Terry Rees. Second row: Colin Spurway, Phillip Gerrard, Brynley Edwards, John Pearce, John Hughes, Roy Frowen, –?–, Alan Poole, Willy Rees, Frankie Rees, Robert Simons, David Lewis. Front row: Kenny Jones, Morgan Llewellyn, Cliff Robbins, Terry Stephens, Geoff Hargest.

Eglwys Newydd Boys' School, 1958. From left to right, back row: Brian Mitchell, Brinley Edwards, Robert Watson, Kenny Jones, Anthony Davis, Dermot Harris, John Davis, Clive Meecham, Terry Rees, Robert Sherlock. Front row: Frank Rees, Willy Rees, Roy Frowen, Phillip Croot, Colin Spurway, Terry Stephens, Allen Pool, John Phillips, Robert Simons, Guy Jennings, John Pearce.

Hawthorn Road Junior School, c. 1960. From left to right, back row: Mr Rees, John Payne, Alan Mitchell, Nigel England, -?-, Christopher Seaman, Peter Wall, Paul Hatfield, -?-, -?-, -?-, Mr Garbut Evans (headmaster). Middle row: John Griffiths, Alan Davies, -?-, Pamela Owen, -?-, -?-, Derek Carew. Front row: Lorna Harries, -?-, -?-, -?-, -?-, Cheryl Legg, Rhoda Phillips, Susan Crumb, -?-, -?-, Angela Roper.

Hawthorn Road Junior School, class 1A, 1962. From left to right, back row: Mr Evans (headmaster), Russell Amos, Robbie Roberts, Stephen Keeling, Gareth Simmonds, Stephen Evans, Peter George, Martin Gallivan, Patrick Whelan, Richard Gardener, Derrick Cosslett, Christopher (?) Lewis, Miss Morris (class teacher). Third row: Bev Canning, Gillian Birch, Sandra Hewitt(?), Edna Davies, Elaine Holbrook, Margaret Perkins, Sylvia Davey, Susan ?, Jackie Orchard, Susan Cook. Second row: Cheryl Shaw, Cheryl ?, Lorraine Hodges, Jennifer Mapstone, Yvonne Holland, -?-, -?-, Karen Joyce, Pat Clements. Front row: Gary Tamplin, Vivian Turley, -?-, Roger Doran, Neil Owen, Christopher Pain.

Whitchurch High School prefects, 1963.

Hawthorn Road Junior School, *c.* 1963. Mr Willis is in the back row, first on the left. Headmaster Garbett Evans on the far right. Standing in the middle row Robert Grice is first on the left. Kenneth Rawlings is third from the left, and Roger Davies is fourth. Richard Sinclair is kneeling down, first on the left.

Hawthorn Road Junior School, *c.* 1964. From left to right, back row: –?–, Nigel Doran, Steve Keeling, Chris Williams, Gareth Simmonds, Richard Gardiner, Russell Amos, Chris Payne, Viv Turley, Robert Roberts. Third row: Gareth Spackman, –?–, –?–, Peter George, Nick Cornish, –?–, Steve Evans, –?–, Paddy Whelan. The names of the girls in the front two rows are not known.

Eglwys Newydd Junior Boys' School, 1964. From left to right, back row: Andrew James, -?-, Emile Borgona, David Lynch, Roger Jones, teacher (name not known). Middle row: David Evans, Mostyn Heard, David Miller, Geoffrey Rice, Brian Tucker, Glyn Thomas, Michael Davies (?), John Parker, Christopher Banks. Front row: Peter Williams, Geoffrey Wyatt, Robert Bosley, David Cox, John Westlake, Mark Jones, Kevin Lord, Stephen Gill, Gordon Thomas, Richard Reeves.

Hawthorn Road Junior School, c. 1967. From left to right, back row: Robert Hartland, Stephen Johnson, Andrew Murphy, Robin Lasbury, Anthony Dungey, Kenneth Price, Sean Cork, Peter Rogers, Mark Jones, David Llewellyn. Middle row: Vicki Lewis, -?-, Wendy Cheeseman, Sandra Lasbury, Sarah Heade, Lucille Symes, Jane Williams, Kim Sugroe, -?-, Judith Marsh, Marcia Stone. Front row: Barbara Evans, Carol James, Debra Cotty, Jane Hopkins, -?-, Mrs Williams (teacher), -?-, Alison York, -?-, Debra Tuthill, Caroline Nash. Sitting: Michael Evans, Glynn Tout, Michael Tout, Stuart Jones.

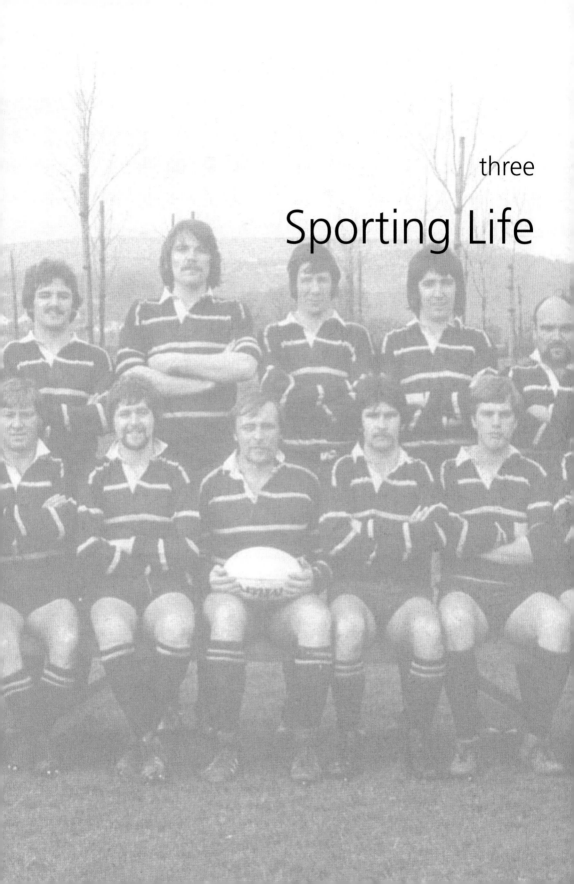

three

Sporting Life

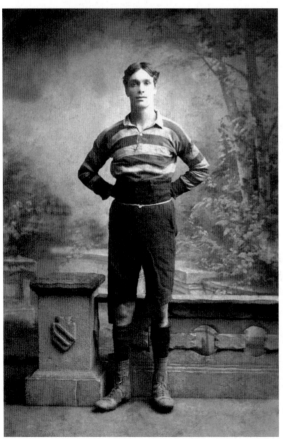

Above: Whitchurch rugby team, 1898/99. From left to right, back row: D. Davies (secretary), C. Samuel, T.L. Williams, T. Harris, D. Chislett, J. Thomas, T. Bennett. Middle row: J.B. Glendenning, F. Cotterell, B. Wiles, T. John, W. Amos, W. Broad, Edmund Boyer, D. Hopkins, G. Bennett (treasurer), E. Townsend. Front row: Cllr J.H. Cory Esq. J.P. (president), T. Llewellyn, D. Rowlands (vice captain), W. Salman (captain), J. Stephens, T. Thompson, E. Evans, Dr I.L. Morris (vice president).

Left: Charles Curtis, Whitchurch rugby player, *c.* 1914.

Whitchurch rugby team, 1920/21. From left to right, back row: D. Jones, E. James, W. Broad, A. Rowlands, J. Evans, L. Lewis, C. Price, W. Salmon, C. Brookman, G. Ronan. Middle row: J. Gibbon, W. Norton, H. Sprudd, T. Jones (vice chairman), J. Coghlan, V. Potter (captain), A. Gibbon, T. Jones, B. Lewis, C. Stockford. Front row: E. Williams, F. Davidson, G. Jones, W. Harwood, H. Jones, H. Lewis, W.G. Jones (hon. sec.), and Master James in front.

Melingriffith Works cricket team, c. 1930.

Above and below: Llandaff North United AFC, *c.* 1930.

The Fox and Hounds skittle team, c. 1930. Trevor Ray is third from the left in the back row, and Arthur Collett is sixth from the left.

The Melingriffith rugby team, *c.* 1937. Holding the rugby ball is Alfred Douglas Clements.

Elyn football team, *c.* 1940. From left to right, back row: Ken Harris, Ted Hopkins, Bryn Dyer, Billy Curtis, Ed Mitchell, Mick Bodman, Dinki Richards, John Jones, J. Curtis, Alf Watkins, D. Howells. Middle row: ? Pope, -?-, Ron Hopkins, T. Humphries, Les Powell. Front row: Les Tucker, Ron Hopkins, Reg Dyer, Ken Hopkins.

Melingriffith rugby team, *c.* 1940. Charlie Clements is in the back row fourth from the left, Alf Clements is sixth from the left, and seventh from the left is Clifford Nicholas.

Above: Hawthorn Road Junior School rugby team, 1946. From left to right, back row: Mr Beckett, Alan Stark, David Roberts, Robert Bush, Donald Hann, Brian Griffiths, Lewis Tucker, Ken Yorath, Raymond Elsworthy, Mr B. Daly. Front row: Trevor Stone, David Llewellyn, Graham Fisher, John Rice, John Clements, Keith Whitcombe, Brian Addicott, John Gibson, Kenneth Griffiths.

Left: John Clements of Llandaff North (centre) and Graham Pymble (right), walking out for Wales at Maindy stadium, *c.* 1950. The name of the man on the left is not known.

John Watkins, Llandaff North
rugby player, c. 1951.

Llandaff North rugby team, 1952. From left to right, back row: Jim Evans, Cliff Day,
Mervyn Richards, Tom Carroll, -?-, John Llewellyn, John Woodward, -?-, Mr McCarthy,
-?-, Trevor Stone, Steve Evans. Middle row: Derek Simmonds, Charlie Rowlands, Derek
Thomas. Front row: John (Gus) Clements, Dennis Alan, Dickie Whitcombe, Pete Watkins,
Roy Davies.

Whitchurch football team, 1955. From left to right, back row: T. Sullivan, -?-, B. Davies, Don Powell, Eric Tucker. Front row: Sid Pritchard, -?-, John Sullivan, Timmy Lynch, Les Davies, Ernie Mitchell, Doug Eckley.

Llandaff North soccer team, c. 1955. From left to right, back row: -?-, -?-, -?-, Alan Bush, Ginger Baker, Jimmy Voisey, Bert ?. Front row: Dennis Leyland, ? Price, Jammy James, Ivor Tout, ? Phelps.

Llandaff North rugby team, 1958. From left to right, back row: Tom Carroll, Viv Jones, ? Beetham, Ian Moffat, David Rose, Rowland Carroll, Dennis Allen, Brian Kempson, Jim Evans, Frank Ward, Bob Evans. Middle row: Graham Beard, Keith Norton, Albert Powell, John Weaver, Jim Wiggins, John Stevens. Front row: Nobby Richards, Jim McCarthy, Gordon Urcombe, D. Powell, Mac Baker.

Llandaff North Rugby Club skittle team, c. 1960. Charlie Bodman is holding the trophy. Also pictured are Johnny Ward, Billy Curzon, Alf Boyer, Ray Allsopp, Colin Bennett, Graham Paton, Jim Evans, Fred Turner and George Tibbett.

The Royal Exchange skittle team, *c*. 1960. From left to right, back row: Dingo Clements, Jim McCarthy, Charley Rowlands, Ginger Jones, Buller Wright. Middle row: Cliff Nicholas, Ivor Lewis, Tommy Rice, Jim Yorath, Tom Thomas, Alf Clements. Front row: Charley Thomas, Ted Lee, Curly Jones, John Jones, Charley Shepard.

Whitchurch football team, *c*. 1960. From left to right, back row: Mr Bayliss, Dai Goddard, Dickie Fairchild, -?-, Gerald Thomas, Brian Light, Jack Tribie, -?-. Front row: John Davies, Dai Cousins, Jeff Rowley, Kenny Light, Peter Dowling, Des Rowley.

Llandaff North RFC Youth, 1966. From left to right, back row: Tony Leaves, Les Traynor, Jeff Wilson , A. Norton, Hank Wheeler, Tony Trigg, C. Tucker, Peter Whitcombe. Middle row: J. Ward, Steve Tibbatts, Phil Xerri, Alfie Hall, J. Wall, R. Carroll, Bob Chard. Front row: Alyn Thomas, Dickie Davey, Clive Stockdale, Andy Church.

Opposite above: The Royal Exchange skittle team, *c.* 1960.

Opposite below: Whitchurch Grammar School under 15's rugby team, *c.* 1962. From left to right, back row: Tony Rowley, Wayne Stratton, –?–, –?–, Gwyn Bowden, –?–, –?–. Middle row: Roger Marriott, David Richards, Fred Reynolds, –?– (captain), Peter Lewis, Dilwyn Stool, –?–. Front row: Alun Rees, –?–, Brian Mitchell, Paul Catterson.

The Legion Extras skittle team, *c.* 1965. From left to right, back row: Ray John, Colin ?, Alan Thomas, Roy James, Glyn (Harry) Ford, Cyril Harman, Cyril Holloway, Jeff Rowley, Cyril Herbert, Colin Light. Middle row: Bill Ford, Dougie Beaumont, Harry Hill. Front row: Mac Ford, John Thomas, Dai Light, Norton Smith, Kenny Paul.

Whitchurch Rugby Football Club baseball team, *c.* 1971. From left to right, back row: E. Davies, A. Davies. Middle row: C. Clark, H. Lansdown, Ian Moffatt, G. Probert, B. Carter, P. Lewis, R. Flay. Front row: F. Lansdown, Brian Light, Jeff Day, Graham Ford, Kevin Lord, T. Smith, Tommy Crews.

The Ladybirds skittle team, champions in 1972. From left to right: Mo Moss, Marcia Tout, Pat Coleman, Eileen Mitchell, Mary Vaughan, Jean Quick (almost hidden), Ann Freeman, Mo Tout (at rear), Nancy Lane, Mary Mitchell, Beatie Croot, Joan Doubler(?) Glenys Vaughan.

Eglwys Newydd Boys' School cricket team, *c.* 1972. From left to right, back row: Mr Williams, Mike Jones, Richard Thomas, Chris Fennessey, Mr Davies. Middle row: Richard Leyshon, Gareth Jones, Steven Bromley, Peter Morris, Mike Eklund, Tony Munday, Phil Townsend. Front row: Owen Phipps, Chris Pike, Dai Kenning, Kevin Beard, Kevin Thomas.

Whitchurch Youth Club football team, *c.* 1978. From left to right, back row: Nigel Hinton, Tony Milsom, Kevin Hollingsworth, Martin Lockwood, Anthony Carey, Alan Mitchell, Russell Winstanley. Front row: Nigel Attwell, Kevin Lane, Gareth Joslim, Kim Provis, Jeff McCue.

Whitchurch Rugby Football Club women's skittles team, *c.* 1975. From left to right: Rose Davies, Irene Isaac, Flo Deacy, Betty Lewis, Margaret Blight, Pat Canavan, Ricky Lock, Janet Clarf, Brenda Deacy, Shirley Cox, Dolly Callnon, Hazel Batten.

Llandaff North rugby team, *c.* 1979. From front to back: Clive Richards, Eric James, Geoff Wilson and Keith Davies.

Llandaff North rugby team First XV 1979/80. From left to right, back row: Chris Powell, Keith Edwards, John Knight, Graham Busfield, Geoff Wilson. Middle row: Glyn Davies, Martin Bray, Ken Price, Gareth Williams. Front row: Martin Davies, John Hill, Micky Dwyer, Phil Morgan, Steve Fish, Dave Evans, Howard Slade.

Llandaff North rugby team, *c.* 1977. From left to right, back row: Eric Raffle, Tony Furnham, -?-, Paul Westaway, Keith Davies, Clive Richards, -?-, Richard Baldwin, Phil Morgan, Terry Milford. Front row: Lyn Joyce, Terry McCarthy, Alun Thomas, Alf Hall (captain), John Leaves, Kelvin Hare, Mervyn Tout(?), Chris Ball.

Above: Whitchurch Rugby Football Club snooker team 1984/85. From left to right, standing: Tony Cartwright, A. Booy, Jock Lewis, N. Chivers, Jeff Day, Bobby Dunlop. Sitting: Brian Light, Ron Hopkins, Mal Robbins, Glyn Davies, Tommy Crews, Sam Parker.

Left: Emma Davies, granddaughter of Whitchurch resident George Morris, is pictured here in the 800m semi-final at the Commonwealth Games in Kuala Lumpur in 1998.

four

People at
Work and Play

Sergeant Major Charles Burley Ward, born 10 July 1877, was decorated with the Victoria Cross at Windsor Castle on 15 December 1900; his was the last Victoria Cross to be presented by Queen Victoria. Citation in the *London Gazette* on 28 September 1900 read:

On 26th June 1900 at Lindley, a piquet of the Yorkshire Light Infantry was surrounded on 3 sides by about 500 Boers at close quarters. The two officers were wounded and all but six of the men killed or wounded. Pte Ward then volunteered to take a message asking for reinforcements to the signaling station about 150 yards in the rear of the post. His offer was at first refused owing to the practical certainty of him being shot, but on his insisting, he was allowed to go. He got across untouched through a storm of shots from each flank and, having delivered his message, he voluntarily returned from a place of absolute safety and re-crossed the fire swept ground to assure his CO that the message had been sent. On this occasion he was severely wounded. But for this gallant action the post would certainly have been captured.

Charles Burley Ward died on 30 December 1921 and was buried at St Mary's churchyard on Church Road. A series of events was organized by the British Legion Earl Haig Club to mark the unveiling of a War Grave Commission style headstone in his memory.

Glamorgan Special Constabulary (Whitchurch) 1914–17. Harry J. Gillett is standing in the middle row, seventh from the left.

Railway employees, *c.* 1920. Trevor Ray is in the back row, fourth from the left.

Employees of the Taff Vale Railway based at Radyr Yard, *c.* 1920. William Nicholas is in the centre. The K class engine was built for the Taff Vale Railway in 1884 and was used mainly for coal traffic to and from the Rhondda, Merthyr and Aberdare valleys.

Co-op annual outing, *c.* 1927. Philip Henry Blakemore and his mother Mary Elizabeth Blakemore (*née* Golding) are sitting directly above the rear wheel.

The wedding of David Lewis Rowlands at the Royal Exchange, 1927. Included in the front row are, from left to right, Doris Rowlands, Florence Ada Soule, David Lewis Rowlands, Emma Eliza Samuel, Ada Hannah Steele. In the middle row, third from the left, is David Rowlands (the groom's father), Blanche Ada Clements is next but one, Margaret Rowlands is second from the right, Charles Price, and Violet Rowlands. In the back row on the far right are Augustas Charles Clements and Mrs Boyer.

Llandaff North charabanc outing, c. 1930. Standing in front of the bus, first and second on the left, are Margaret Ann Nicholas and Mrs Boyer. On-board the bus behind Margaret Ann Nicholas are Margaret Sarah Nicholas and Fanny Maud Nicholas.

Left: Reg and Iris Cox outside their parents' shop in Blosse Road, *c.* 1931.

Below: Employees of the Melingriffith Tinplate Works, June 1934.

The Masons Arms, 1937. Some people pictured here include C. Drucker, \N. Burke, Tom O'Keefe, Bill Lane, Mr Bodman, Mr Rowley, Mr Jones, Ernie Mitchell, Mr Kidwell, Mr Grimshaw, Alf Grimshaw, Mr Lane, Ted Bodman, Ivor Fields.

3rd Whitchurch Girl Guides, *c.* 1938. From left to right, back row: Hazel Davies, -?-, Phyllis Jennett, Veronica Thomas, Betty Thompson, -?-, -?-, -?-, -?-, -?-, -?-, -?-. Middle row: Mary Samuel, -?-, Joyce Griffiths, Yvonne Griffiths, Lieutenant Jo Pryce, Captain Olwen Morgan, Margaret Griffiths, Joyce Wild, Moira Ford, Dilys ?, Iris Cox. Front row: -?-, -?-, -?-, Barbara Gould, -?-, Jean Griffiths, -?-, -?-, -?-, -?-.

No. 3 Platoon, Llandaff North Home Guard, *c.* 1940. From left to right, back row: Courtney Rowlands, -?-, Sam Troake, -?-, -?-, -?-, Len Wright, Charlie Barry, George Tucker, -?-, -?-, Ted Woodward, Trevor Mullins, Ike Stephens, Frank Jago Ward, -?-, -?-. Middle row: Tom Richards, Eddie Evans, George Hann, Dai Rowlands, -?-, -?-, Rupert Evans, -?-, Gordon Tout, -?-, Jack Hobbs, -?-, Len Tout, -?-, Charlie Bodman, -?-, -?-. Front row: -?-, -?-, -?-, -?-, -?-, -?-, -?-, -?-, Sgt Grimshaw, -?-, -?-, -?-, -?-, Pete Watkins, -?-, -?-, -?-, -?-.

Llandaff North ladies outing, *c.* 1940. From left to right, back row: Mrs Lee,
Mrs Jones, Olive Whitcombe, Mrs Colinson, -?-, -?-, -?-, Mrs Lee, -?-, Mrs Thomas,
Gwen Lee. Middle row: Mrs Whitcombe, -?-, Mrs Yard, Mrs Dean, -?-, -?-, -?-. Front
row: Mrs Lee, Mrs Clements, Mrs Lodge, Mrs Stone, -?-, Naomi Robbins, -?-, -?-,
Mrs Howe, -?-, -?-, -?-.

Tom Wonnacott, landlord of the Railway Hotel, Llandaff North, *c.* 1940.

Left: Employees of the Melingriffith Tinplate Works, *c.* 1940. From left to right, back row: Charlie Larcombe, Sid Abbott, Tom Robins, Johnny Yorath. Front row: Steve Evans, Buller Wright, Stan Blakemore, Ted Phillips.

Below: Whitchurch Home Guard, *c.* 1940. Howard Cousins is second from the left in the back row, fourth is Ernie Mitchell, and eighth is Timmy Burke. Sergeant Lewis is ninth from the left in the middle row.

Whitchurch Methodist young wives, *c.* 1940.

VE Day party in 1945 at Ararat church. Catherine Jones is first on the left in the middle row. Martin Hughes is fifth from the left, Marion Hughes is on Martin's right, Charles Wyatt is seventh from the left, and Hugh Jones is eighth from the left. Tudor Jones is seventh from the left in the back row.

Above and below: Heol Booker VE Day street party and children's fancy dress, 1945.

Nicholls and Winfield Victoria Laundry van, *c.* 1950.

Opposite above: Nicholls and Winfield Victoria Laundry van drivers, *c.* 1950. The boys were known as van boys and helped the driver.

Opposite below: Employees of Victoria Laundry totalling 496 years of service, *c.* 1950. On the far right is Ivor Nicholls. Names include Arthur Tripp, Bill Witlock, Ron Wood, A. Paul, Cliff Tucker, Bob Steel, Trevor Lewis and Maggie Rowlands.

Plough skittle outing, *c.* 1948. From left to right: Billy Davies, Herbie Perkins, Charlie Hutton, Tommy Fields, -?-, Ernie Mitchell, Tommy Perkins, Mr Phelan, Eddie Mitchell, Eddie Roberts, Ken Jenkins, -?-, -?-, Bill Lane, Bill Davies, -?-, -?-, Joe Hughs, Harry Stafford (sitting), -?-, landlord of the Plough, Cyril Harman, -?-, -?-, -?-, -?-, -?-, Dai Hartree, Mr Harman, -?-, -?-, Bernard Mitchell, Mr Richards, -?-, Reggie Bodman.

Talbot A. Gardiner, transport contractor, Whitsun Monday, 1946. Mary Gardiner is third from the left, and Talbot Gardiner is sixth from the left.

Victoria Laundry outing on the corner of Andrews Road, Llandaff North, *c.* 1950. Janet Lee is fourth from the left in the back row; Fred Collings is eighth from the left. Margaret Lee is fifth from the left in the front row.

The 21st Cardiff Company of the Boys' Brigade held a parents evening at their headquarters at Ararat Baptist church, Whitchurch, 1951. The photograph shows the company after the presentation of badges and awards by Mr W.H. Miller, chairman of the Cardiff Battalion. From left to right, front row: Cpl B. Thomas, Lt L. Thomas, Revd W. George Evans (chaplain), Capt. T. Catterson, Capt. W.H. Miller, Lt P.G. Evans, Lt C.K. Davies, L/Cpl R. Lloyd and Cpl C. Gardener.

Billy Watkins, Sammy Curtis, Reg Watkins and Margaret Cousins, c. 1950.

Heol Don Queen Elizabeth II Coronation street party, 1953. At the back on the left are Nurse Green and Margaret Edmonds. In front of Nurse Green is Yvonne Osborne. At the back on the right is Joy Luck. The two boys to the left of Joy Luck are Dougie and Cyril Holloway.

Queen Elizabeth II Coronation street party, West Road, 1953. From left to right are Linda Jones, Lorna Jones, Geoffrey Jones and Dulcie Hann.

Queen Elizabeth II Coronation street party, West Road, 1953. From left to right:
George Humphries, Mrs King, Gordon Hann and Gordon Hann Junior.

Queen Elizabeth II Coronation street party, West Road, 1953. At the back are Gordon
Hann and George Humphries. In front are Howard Gill, Glyn Howells, Gordon Hann,
? Norris and ? Norris.

3rd Whitchurch Grammar School Scout Troop, 1957. From left to right, back row: -?-, -?-, Rhys Jones, Cyril Williams, David Morris, -?-, -?-, Peter Ferda, -?-, -?-. Fourth row: Paul Salmon, -?-, -?-, son of Pentyrch Rector, -?-, -?-, -?-, -?-, Bob Howells, -?-, -?-. Third row: -?-, Clive Gronow, -?-, Haydn Gigg, Barry Thomas, Bob ?, -?-, Peter Snyder, -?-, Nigel Graves. Second row: Roger Owens, -?-, David Barry, Tim Stamps, Gordon Richards, Len Manaton, Tim Pollard, David Perry, David Phillips, Chris Light, Gwyn Laviers. Front row: -?-, -?-, Little Beetham, David Cogar, -?-, -?-, -?-, ? Upstall, -?-, Peter Crook, -?-, -?-.

Ted Hayman, an employee of Saturn Industrial Gases, with his Ford 100E van, *c*. 1958.

A group of GKN Sankey employees, *c.* 1960. Terry Kidner is second from the left in front row, and Harry Hill is first from the left in the second row.

The plating workshop at GKN Sankey where car bumpers were manufactured and chromium plated, *c.* 1960.

Alfred Douglas Clements (left) of Ty Mawr Road, *c.* 1960. Alfred was employed as a blacksmith on the railways, working out of the Salisbury Road depot on the Cardiff to the Valleys lines. On the right is striker Tommy Thompson.

Opposite above: Regulars enjoying a good night at the Royal Exchange, *c.* 1960.

Opposite below: A works party at GKN Sankey, *c.* 1960. Mac Ford is fourth from the left, Joyce Paul is fifth, Gladys Farnham is seventh, and Stan Jones, with daughter Ann Jones, is eleventh.

2nd Llandaff Scouts at Treguf Farm between Bonvilston and Llancarfan, 1961. From left to right, back row: Paul Donovan, -?-, Kelvin Dean, Peter Gage and Buster Ware. Front row: Ronnie Carrol, John Jugessur, -?-, Paul Wilkins, -?- (formerly of Colwinstone Street, Llandaff North), -?- (District Commissioner at the time), Michael Bates.

Cow and Snuffers outing, 1962. Some of the people pictured here include Ken Howe Senior, Danny Howells, Jack Collins (landlord of Cow and Snuffers), Jack Gosling, Len Davey, Little Willy, Fred Lloyd, Trevor Tucker, Phil Tucker, Kenneth Howe Junior, Bill Hillard, Phil Jones. Raymond George Martin is in the front row, first on the left.

Above: Children from Heol Booker and Heol Penlan, *c.* 1966. Some of the kids pictured here include Margaret Farnham, Elaine James, Phillip Parker, Alan Mitchell, Beasie Bale, Macky Bale, Butchy Bale, Howard Evans, Terry Kidner, Dai Mitchell, Dai Jones, Tina James and Colin Griffiths.

Right: Whitchurch Rugby Club Grog Trot, *c.* 1968. On the left is Johnny Hopkins and on the right is Willy Rees.

Reunion of former employees of the Melingriffith Tinplate Works at Taffswell Rugby Club, *c.* 1970. On the right is Mrs Florence Thomas, the only woman present. Others pictured here include Albert Gaylard, Edward Thomas, Edward Phillips, Reg Phillips, (back row, centre) and Clifford Nicholas (second row, third from the right).

Children from Heol Booker enjoying a day out at Tongwynlais Park, *c.* 1970. From left to right, front row: Glyn Nicholas, Ann Calway, Angela Farnham, Janet Farnham, David Nicholas. Middle row: Kevin Kidner, Terence Kidner, Jane Paul, Margaret Farnham. Back row: Brenda Kidner.

Whitchurch Rugby Club pensioners' outing, *c.* 1970. From left to right, front row: -?-, -?-, Harry Larkin, -?-, Harry Lambert, -?-, -?-, Ginger Roberts, -?-, -?-. Eleventh from the left, back row: Aggie Tout, Gordon Tout, -?-, Hector Sims, -?-, Mrs Pearce, Hannah Farnham, Mrs Watkins, Gladys Parker, Minnie Harman, Chrissie Parker.

Whitchurch pensioners' outing to Great Yarmouth, *c.* 1970. Some of the people pictured here include Minnie Harman, Aggie Tout, Mrs Mitchell, Mrs Morgan, Beatie Croot, Lillian Tout, Mrs Gibbon, Harry Lambert, Hannah Farnham, Ivor Tout and Gordon Tout.

Whitchurch Rugby Football Club committee, 1971/72. From left to right, back row: Sam Parker, Graham Ford, P. Lewis, Ray Vaughan, E. Roberts, G. Probert, G. Donne. Front row: Russell Lord, Jeff Day (vice chairman), Viv Pearce, Brian Light (chairman), Tommy Crews (secretary), Peter Mann.

Opposite above: The Pineapple outing, 1973. Some of the people here include Jim Paice, Ezzie ?, Danny ?, Sidney Owen, Georgie and Jeffrey Britton, Randall Chapman, Peter Chessman, Paul Timothy, Ken Howe, Ken Howe Junior, Johnny Morgan, Douggie Gougie, Ken Chard, Douggie Price, Mickey Green.

Opposite below: Atlas Express employees, c. 1975. From left to right: Martin Wyatt, Ken ?, -?-, Albert Griffiths, Eddie Westlake, Phil Maidment, Fred Turi, John Jones, Lawrence Gulley, -?-, Robert Whitten, Lance Almond.

Whitchurch Coronets jazz band at Mynachdy Institute, November 1976. Names include Dai Rowley, David Nicholas, Neil Griffiths, Janet Farnham, Glyn Nicholas, Robert Bagley, Jeff Robbins, Robert Rowley, Alison Pound, Wendy Robbins, Charlie Stickler, Julie Mitchell, Katie Dunlop, Jane Wheadon,

Christine Pound, Jane Dyer, Karen Bagley, Samantha Donovan, Angela Farnham, Beverley Rayer, Julie Bagley, Kim Robbins, Ann Calway, Rhiannon Evans, Leanne Farnham, Susan Bagley, Debbie James, Rosalyn Evans.

Ty Mawr Road council depot, *c.* 1985. From left to right, front row: Terry Williams, Tony Morgan, Terry Kidner. Back row: Dave Atkins, John Feruji, Rob Light, Trevor Davies, Mark Yule, Mike Spears, Derek Rogers, Boyo Ale, Fred Ellis, Mac McCarthy, Mike O'Sullivan, Dave Equals, Ken McCarthy, Mervyn Prosser.

Opposite above: The skittle team and regulars of the Pineapple, *c.* 1976. Holding the newspaper is Ray Martin.

Opposite below: Atlas Express employees, 1984. From left to right: Lance Almond, Ken ?, Willy Rees, Fred Turi, Richie Brown, Ian Campbell, Dai Nicholas, Phil Maidment, Albert Griffiths, Jack Ashley, Ken Weslake, Eric Ellis, Lawrence Gully, Martin Wyatt, David Nicholas, Tony Madley, George Light, Percy Ford, Billy Trigg, Tony Witts, Wayne Eglen.

Whitchurch Coronets jazz band, *c.* 1985. From left to right, back row: Siân Sweeney, Joanne Sanders, Neil Griffiths, Robert Rowley, Dai Rowley, Angie Farnham. Middle row: Leslie-Anne Sanders, Rhiannon Sweeney, Alison Drew, Nadine Morrell, Julie Light, Michelle Salamon, Janine Rees, Angela Morgan, Julie Griffiths. Front row: Catherine Sweeney, Debbie ?, Tara Sweeney, Sharon Drew, Paula Rees, Naomi Carroll.

Leo's Lions jazz band, 1983. From left to right, back row: Cheryl Whittaker, Michelle Campbell, Gaynor Hathoway, Suzanne Powell, Michelle Crook, Rhian Davies. Third row: Charlie Bennett, Alison Pound, Maria Debono, Carol Campbell, Ann-Marie Henderson, Liz Stevens, Mandy Rogers, Helen Day, Patti Russell. Second row: Tony Ann James, -?-, Gaynor Hathoway, Jane Phipps, Claire Louise Davies, Alison Davies. Front row: Michelle Ellis, Yvonne James, Tracey McCarthy, Joanne Day.

Whitchurch Male Voice Choir, 1993.

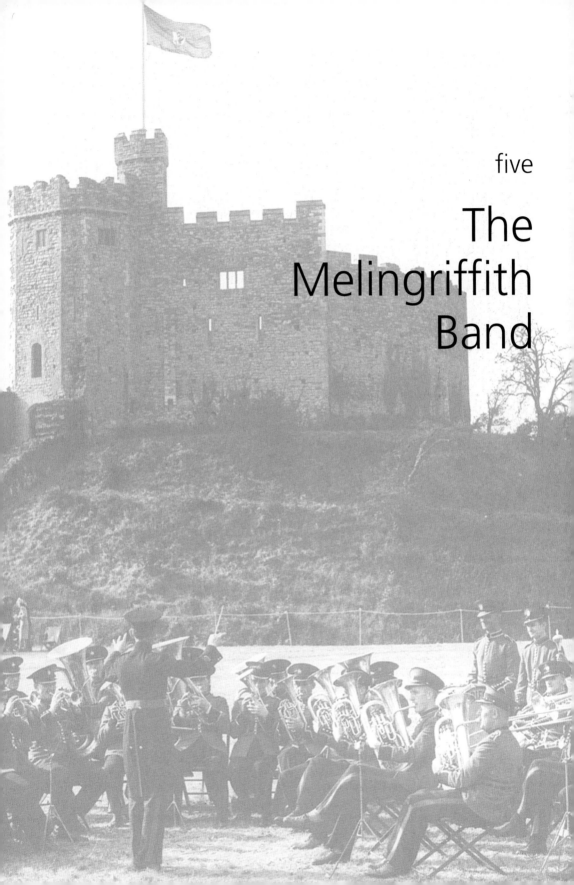

five

The Melingriffith Band

Thomas James Powell (12 October 1897 – 29 January 1965).

A tribute by E. Vaughan Morris in *The Conductor* magazine, April 1965: 'T.J. Powell: A mighty friend'. W.G. Atkins September 1969

T.J. (Tom) Powell was born in Tredegar, Monmouthshire, on 12 October 1897 to Edgar and Sarah Anne Powell. As has been the case with many musicians in the brass band movement, he started as a boy in the Salvation Army, and was playing side-drum in the youth band at the age of seven. He transferred to the Tredegar Senior Band on cornet and studied theory and harmony during this period with Mr Hurley, who was Bandmaster there. Just prior to the First World War, he joined the Tredegar Town Band but then left South Wales to serve with distinction in the Band of HM Royal Marines; he furthered his studies during the war in the Marines School of Music. In 1920 he was appointed Musical Director of the Melingriffith Volunteer and Cadet Corps Band which was connected to the Melingriffith Tinplate Works at Whitchurch, just outside Cardiff; he lived locally for many years at No. 81 Velindre Road, Whitchurch. This was the beginning of an association which lasted all his life, and the names of 'Melingriffith' and 'Tom Powell' will be forever linked together. He conducted with Mr Tom Moore – a top cornet with Besses of the Barn – who had been coaching the band in those early days and within three years the band progressed very rapidly from Class C to Class A. At the same time he coached the Cardiff Transport Band and had quite some successes with them. Over the years the Melingriffith Band grew in reputation with Tom Powell conducting, and T.J. eventually came to adjudicate all over the country and was in great demand as a coach, despite the fact that he never advertised.

Composing was a great joy to him. Early in his career with Melingriffith he wrote a March called 'Appreciation', dedicated to Mr David Millward who was secretary of the band at the time and who helped Tom in his early days. He excelled at writing Marches and 'Appreciation' was a forerunner of more than fifty. Some have never been printed, but are on manuscript in the library of the Excelsior Ropes Band who succeeded Melingriffith on the closing of the Tinplate Works. Many of the Marches were named after Welsh castles – Castell Coch (the Red Castle), which was visible from his home, and Castell Caerdydd (Cardiff Castle) and Castell Caerphilli (Caerphilly Castle) were close by. 'Caernarfon Castle' was written in 1958 when HM the Queen announced that Prince Charles was to be made Prince of Wales. His March the 'Contestor' has been recorded by Black Dyke Mills, amongst many others. Harry Mortimer once referred to him as the 'Welsh Sousa'. He also composed many selections, waltzes, studies and solos, to his credit; he arranged many pieces for brass band, including a complete book of Welsh hymns.

T.J. Powell's works are often broadcast and frequently used as test pieces. There are some interesting anecdotes about the inspiration for some of his works, for example 'Snowdon Fantasy' was written by Tom following a visit to Snowdonia with Mr Hughes – a North Wales Bandmaster who lived at the foot of the mountain. 'Forest Bells' was inspired by the pealing of church bells in the Forest of Dean when he was walking through the Forest to rehearse Pillowell Band there. He wrote many pieces for solo instruments with Bank accompaniment: his quintet 'The Tops' is a favourite of many bands. Some works were composed specifically for particular Melingriffith bandsmen, and for want of titles he reversed their surnames – thus 'Snikta' is an Eb Bass Theme and variations, while 'Elyod' a euphonium solo and variations. He was an exceedingly quick writer of manuscripts; he would often try out an idea on the piano, and have full band parts and score ready by the next rehearsal.

He received many honours. He was presented to HRH Princess Marina by the South Wales & Monmouthshire St Johns' Ambulance Brigade function in Caerphilli when he was awarded a medal for loyal services to the Ambulance Brigade and for several years he was president of the South Wales & Monmouthshire Brass Band Association. He was invited to conduct at many important functions with the National Brass Band. He was one of the few holders of the Silver Medal of the Worshipful Company of Musicians of London, presented to him at Belle Vue in 1958. He was presented with the Diploma of Honour of the NBCCC of Great Britain. As an ex-Marine he was always spick and span and expected his band to be likewise. Mr Alan Spence-Thomas (whose family owned the Melingriffith Works) was a Captain in the Welsh Guards and he designed the MGB uniform to be similar to the Guards. He too was insistent that the Band should be well turned out for all occasions, and over the years many prizes were won for marching and deportment – more often than not marching in one of T.J.'s compositions. Tom Powell inspired all who were around him and commanded their great respect as conductor and composer and also in his qualities as gentleman and friend. His tragic death on 29 January 1965, whilst guest conducting the Cory Band, brought to an end a life which had been spent in ungrudging service to others. The brass band movement lost a champion. Undoubtedly Wales' 'Man of Brass'.

T.J. Powell started his musical career as a boy in the Salvation Army band, and was playing side–drum in the youth band at the age of seven. This postcard of the Salvation Army band came from T.J. Powell's own collection of memorabilia. He is seen here in the back row, far right.

Whitchurch Brass Band, 18 September 1908. From left to right, back row: ★T. Bodger, ★Callaway Smith, ★E.C. Smith, W. Nicholas, T. Fuse. Middle row: W. Thomas, T. Richards, T. Howells, S. Fuse, ★A. Villa, ★F. Smith, B. Smith, F. Morgan (chairman), J. Morgan. Front row: Aubrey J. Morgan (secretary), ★P. Collins, E. Billing, Mr J. Chivers (conductor), ★T.H. Collins, A. Baker, Arthur Morgan (treasurer), D. Thomas. (★Members of Committee)

The Melingriffith Band in 1923.

The Melingriffith Volunteer and Cadet Corps Band, 1928. From left to right, back row: H. Brown (Librarian), C. Smith, E. Morgan (Deputy Bandmaster and Hon. Treasurer), I. Rich, W. Williams, J. Woollen, N. Rees, T. Fuse, T. Grimshaw. Middle row: J.B. Smith, B. Smith, S. Grimshaw, H. Tansley, A. Doyle, S. Howells, E. Hole, A. Davey. Front row: A. Morgan, H. Grimshaw, T. Addicott, J. Brown, T.J. Powell (Bandmaster), C. Doyle, R. Brown, T. Atkins, P. Nibblet, C. Luce, H. Evans (Assistant Secretary).

It was during 1937 that the Melingriffith Band, upon the instigation of the then president Mr Alan Spence-Thomas, adopted their now-famous scarlet Welsh Guards pattern uniform, and one of the first things to do was have their photograph taken on the steps of the County Hall in Cardiff.

Some history of the Melingriffith Band taken from T.J. Powell's Annual Report for 1949:

It has occurred to me that, as we have quite a number of new members it would be a good thing to say something about the history of our band. I think it is a fine thing when one knows just what lies behind any cause for which one works and strives especially if, by knowing, one can realise a source of pride and pleasure from such knowledge. If I can convey to you, in part at least, the past of this band I feel sure we will all find both pride and pleasure in our connection with it. How far back in history it goes we are not quite able to say – but it is fairly certain that it goes back a hundred years at least. We have heard that it was originally a drum and fife band, later becoming a sort of semi-military in the days when the works were owned by a family called Booker. It seems that in some ways the band was then on a similar basis to the present day Foden's in as much that the main interest of the employer owner family was in the men's ability to play in the band. The players were very often at the boss's house playing instead of at work. There is no evidence though of any strides having been made outside of their locality at Melingriffith. Eventually the band left the environment of the works and became Whitchurch Brass Band and flourished quite well for many years having some well known men of that day as conductor players, such as James Livesay of the famous Cyfartha band family and Elias Billings one of the leading cornet players of his time. These two men were still about when I came to Melingriffith in 1920, thirty years ago. I can give you a much better picture from then of course. I found a band of 11 players when I came, little or no funds, in the main a poor lot of instruments, a library which had hardly an item complete and uniforms for some and not for others. You must remember that there had been a break in the activity during 1914-1918 war. What I did find here was plenty of enthusiasm and a tremendous willingness to be led. I knew very little about the running of a band on amateur lines, but we got down to work and in 6 months had a full band, the following year entering the first contest. It will be of interest to you to know that, in our ignorance of band matters, we found we had entered a class 'B' contest and were up against bands like 'Cory's' and Aberaman, who were class 'B' bands at that time. You don't need me to tell you we were placed last. However, 6 months later, having to drop players to compete, on account of the numbers restriction we registered our first win gaining first prize at Treorchy in a class 'C' contest. Mr Jimmy Roberts was our coach, acting over me as I would now act over BM of say Pillowell. I wasn't quite happy about him though as I felt that he was not quite the man we wanted, I wanted tuition too as well as the band and it was arranged to call in Mr T.G. Moore who taught me more in ten minutes than anyone else has in my whole life. We had success with him, but the financial side was poor in those days and we resolved to leave competition and try to build up in other ways. We went out to popularise the band for engagements and succeeded very well indeed being able as a result to obtain good uniforms, instruments and a good library, that this was very much to the good there was no shadow of a doubt for, when we decided to return to the contest field in 1928 nothing could stop us, without a coach or outside help of any sort, starting at Chepstow open contest in 1928 we walked through to class 'A' in three years, and we have stayed there ever since. The amount of work to put in, in those days would hardly be believed and how necessary it all was is apparent when I tell you that I can remember an annual meeting such as this when our funds showed a credit balance of 9d. Quite a different story of today. The building up of equipment has been a very hefty job and I would like the younger people realise that, easy as it seems now to be equipped with uniform, instrument, Music, given decent transport to jobs, paid lost time and indeed having everything made as comfortable as possible is only the result of very hard work in the past. It was in 1931 that we first broadcast. For 25 years this has been the foremost band in Cardiff District, having played for Royalty and all big public functions more than any other band can claim. Just one other thing in this very brief run over the past. In 1950 I find myself the oldest member as far as the playing membership goes, with one exception, Dick Brown, who was a member when I came. With that I am afraid, very sketchy run into the past I come to the report for 1949.

CARDIFF CIVIL DEFENCE WELFARE COMMITTEE.
Chairman: Councillor D. ALLAN ROBSON, J.P.

Reardon Smith Lecture Theatre
Tuesday, April 20th, 1943

PROGRAMME—By

MELINGRIFFITH WORKS BAND
(CONDUCTOR - T. J. POWELL).
ACCOMPANIST - T. W. MILLAR.

1. March ... "Light of Heart" ... *T. J. Powell*

2. Overture "Poet and Peasant" ... ... *Suppe*

3. Song ... Selected. ... ...
(Musician T. N. Rees)

4. Cornet Duet ... "Ida and Dot" ... ... *Losey*
(Musicians W. Thomas and J. Hurman)

5. Selection ... The Student Prince" ... ... *Romberg*

6. Trombone Solo "The Acrobat" ... *Greenwood*
(Soloist, H. Morgan)

7. Vocal Duet "Watchman! What of the Night" ... *Sargent*
(Musicians T. N. Rees and T. J. Powell)

8. Selection ... "Community Land" ... ... *Stodden*

9. Trombone Quartette "The North Wind"... ... *Rimmer*

10. An Arrangement of "The White Cliffs of Dover"
Arr. Mackenzie

11. E. Flat Bass Solo "Snikta" ... *T. J. Powell*
(Soloist, G. Atkins)

12. Song ... Selected ... ...
(Musician T. N. Rees)

13. Euphonium Solo "Mother Machree" ... *Arr. T. J. Powell*
(Soloist, H. Pope).

14. Scotch Novelty "Swing o' the Kilt" *Quentin Maclean*

GOD SAVE THE KING.

Melingriffith Works Band programme at Reardon Smith Lecture Theatre, 20 April 1943.

Melingriffith Band at Home Guard sports day, Whitchurch Grammar School field, 14 June 1943. From left to right, back row: J. Atkins, T. Bravery, N. Rees, W. Williams, W. Hocking, J. Brown, R. Squires, A. Cosh, -?-, F. Jones, J. Shepstone, H. Atkins. Front row: G. Atkins, J. Hurman, W. Parkins, W .Thomas, R. Oliver, T.J. Powell, E. Baker, J. Moore, A. Atkins, H. Morgan, A. Morgan.

T.J. Powell rehearses the Melingriffith Band prior to their visit to the Welsh Industries Fair in London, 1947. At this time, the band room was the old Whitchurch piggery near Ty Mawr farm.

Above and below: T.J. Powell leads the Melingriffith Band at celebrations for the handover of Cardiff Castle to the City by the Marquis of Bute in 1948. Under Powell the band became justifiably famous for their marching skill and immaculate turn-out, their high-collared scarlet tunics being modelled on those of the Welsh Guards.

Melingriffith Band, with T.J. Powell, marching through Whitchurch to mark the Coronation of Queen Elizabeth II in 1953.

The Melingriffith Band on the march.

National Eisteddfod, Caerphilly, 1950. From left to right, back row: J. Hurman, W. Ellis, J. Shepstone, W. Thomas, A. Pope, G. Davies, W. Howells, H. Payne. Fourth row: T. Burley, E. Baker. Third row: T.J. Powell, P. Bellringer, J. Atkins, G. Tout, C. Goss, W. Hocking, R. Squires, C. Cawley, A. Atkins. Second row: R. Cruwys, N. Rees, S. Howells, H. Pope, T. Atkins. Front row: H. Jenkins, G. Atkins, F. Jones, R. Brown.

Above: Members of the Melingriffith Band get a pep talk from conductor T.J. Powell before competing in the National Eisteddfod in Singleton Park, Swansea, in August 1964.

Left: Mary Ann Powell and Thomas James Powell, *c.* 1940.

Daily Herald

NATIONAL BRASS BAND
CHAMPIONSHIPS
OF GREAT BRITAIN

FESTIVAL CONCERT

Under the Gracious Patronage of
Her Majesty The Queen

**ROYAL
ALBERT HALL**

(*Manager: C. R. Hopper*)

Saturday, 20th October
1962

1/-

Programme from 20 October 1962 when the Melingriffith Band played at the Albert Hall.

T.J. Powell's home at No. 81 Velindre Road, Whitchurch.

Praise for Powell

MOST cities honour their famous sons in some way or another, yet Cardiff, or more precisely, Whitchurch, has a son whose fame was and remains international wherever musicians come together to play.

He was a prolific composer whose work spans mood and style effortlessly, yet his original work lies neglected.

I refer to the man known affectionately as "the Welsh Sousa" — T J Powell.

For those who don't know the name, T J Powell is one of the greatest British composers of brass music, ranking alongside Rimmer, and was, for many years, conductor of the once great Melingriffth Band.

Isn't it time that we DID honour him? And isn't it time that we made a serious effort to collate and restore his music?

PETER SUNMAN, Boleyn Walk, Penylan, Cardiff

News cutting praising T.J. Powell.

ROYAL NEW ZEALAND AIR FORCE

TELEPHONE: 482.049
Ext 833

RNZAF Base Wigram,
Private Bag,
Christchurch,
NEW ZEALAND.

IN REPLY QUOTE WG 1200/4

2nd June 1983

Mrs. J. King,
58 Heol Penlan,
Whitchurch,
CARDIFF,
S. Glam CF4 2BZ,
WALES.

Dear Mrs. King,

Thank you for your letter of 23rd May 1983 seeking information on the march played by the Wigram Base band during the visit by Their Royal Highnesses The Prince and Princess of Wales.

You are of course correct when you assume that it was a march written by your late father. The name of the march was "Castell Caerffili" and a note to this march was that it was written to commemorate the Welsh National Eisteddfod 1950. "Castell Caerdydd" and "Castel Coch" are two other marches that are very frequently used by our New Zealand bands for contest and concert programmes, and T. J. Powell's music is held in very high regard by our bandsmen in New Zealand.

I trust that this information is helpful to you and I wish you many hours of pleasure listening to your father's music.

Yours faithfully,

Graeme Aldridge

(G. V. ALDRIDGE)
Bandmaster
for Base Commander

A letter to T.J. Powell's daughter, Joyce King, from the Royal New Zealand Air Force, 1983.

Diploma of Honour Award

TOM POWELL

The personal award of a " Diploma of Honour " was instituted last year by the National Brass Band Contesting Council to recognise both lengthy and signal individual service to the brass band movement. Already a number of personalities in the band world have been so honoured.

★   Today, a diploma presentation is to be made in the Royal Albert Hall to 65-year-old Mr. Tom Powell, of Cardiff.

Born in Tredegar, Monmouthshire, he joined the local Salvation Army band as a cornet player at the age of eight. After gaining further playing experience with other bands, he took up conducting, in 1920, with the Melingriffith Band. In addition to his contest success with this band, he has also been called in as trainer by many leading bands in South Wales and the West of England.

★   His wide musical experience includes conducting massed bands concerts, directing at more than 100 band broadcasts, and acting as conductor of the National Brass Band of Wales. A talented writer of band music, quite a number of his compositions, including some stirring marches, have been published.

A respected adjudicator, he has fulfilled responsible appointments all over the country. He has judged at the four Finals of the *Daily Herald* National Brass Band Championships, and today judged the National Second section Championship at the Kensington Town Hall.

Tom Powell receives his Diploma of Honour.

'T.J. Powell: A Mighty Friend', a tribute by E. Vaughan Morris

Goodbye is difficult at any time and in any circumstances. If we accept that it means 'God be with you' it makes it easier to accept that inevitability of the expression. In the case of Tom Powell, with abruptness and no apparent warning, we found it necessary to bid him farewell. Here again, if we can ease our sorrow at the parting in the belief that our muttered and muted salutation means 'Fare Thee Well', the hurt may be lessened in our hearts and minds. Tom was someone very personal to me. Whether he ever wore a mask – which so many of our fellow creatures seem to do – I do not know. To me he was crystal clear and rang true in the manner of his thinking and the nature of his living. There was no artifice in his face, nor in his actions. I honestly believe he was a man imbued with a sense of mission and paramount in his conception was honesty of purpose, untrammeled with self-glorification and self-aggrandizement. I first met him 21 years ago, when he was still sprightly and vigorous to a marked degree. It would be right to say that the Melingriffith Band provided the avenue by which he could give vent to his love and devotion to Brass Band music. There was a combination of respect, affection and utter trust which permeated the atmosphere. In which, the Band and its conductor worked to make music of the highest standard possible. At that time, and for several years afterwards, Tom fronted the Band on its public appearances dressed in the full dress uniform of a Band turned out in impeccable style. He did not ask of his players what he was not prepared to give himself. In the intervening years I had countless opportunities of enjoying a close association with this exceptional and dedicated man. I was privileged to make a contribution towards easing the anxieties and uncertainties with the establishment of the National Brass Band of Wales, which had long been an objective which had animated him until it became a reality. Time and again, he assisted me with that flair and judgment with which he was richly endowed in carrying out adjudication assignments at all levels of the National Brass Band Championships. I was at his side when he was presented at the Royal Albert Hall with the highest accolade of the Brass Band Movement – the Diploma of Honour of the National Brass Band Contesting Council of Great Britain. I had long come to accept him as a friend before whom I could think aloud. He was possessed of a kind of glory which seemed to light up his mind. With the result that he appeared to pour his inner resources and vitality outwards as a torrent which would not be denied and yet he was in nowise diminished. In Tom Powell we had a man of faith. Not for him the barren spending of himself on small matters which had no heart or spirit, tormenting himself over popularity or success, until he had lost the capacity to live each moment to the fullest. I believe that he had – as few men seen to be prepared to do – come into the full realisation of his own awakened internal powers, with the result that he conditioned his Life in strict accord with what he would have it. In taking our farewell of this kind and gracious man, and even accepting the inevitable that the earth gives all and takes all, may we not also think on these lines a person is exactly the same the moment after he as 'died' as he was the moment before. No magical, instantaneous change takes place either in mind, or body. We surely pass on with all our earthly likes and dislikes, all our fancies and foibles all our idiosyncrasies and all our errors fast upon us. If we are just as we were on earth, and it is reasonable that we behave as we did on earth, then we may think and take consolation from the true picture of himself as he really was which our friend Tom Powell will reflect for all time. I shall miss you sorely, good and understanding friend – when occasion permits commune with us so that we continue to feel the warmth of your presence. Farewell!

Other local titles published by Tempus

Rhiwbina
KEN GRAHAM AND JIM TAVERNER

This absorbing collection of over 190 postcards and photographs, many never before published, offers a nostalgic glimpse into the history of Rhiwbina during the last century. Aspects of everyday life are featured, from schools and churches, public houses and shops – such as Tucker the grocer and Lewis the butcher, both situated on Beulah Road in the 1930s – to transport, leisure pursuits and the local residents who proudly call Rhiwbina their home.

0 7524 3299 0

Treforest, Glyntaff and Rhydyfelin
RHODRI JOHN POWELL

This fascinating collection of over 200 old photographs traces the changes that have taken place in Treforest, Glyntaff and Rhydyfelin since the nineteenth century. The Treforest Industrial Estate and the South Wales and Monmouthshire School of Mines are featured and the influence of local figures such as Francis Crawshay and William Price recalled. *Treforest, Glyntaff and Rhydyfelin* will delight all those know this area of South Wales.

0 7524 3507 8

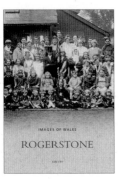

Rogerstone
KIM FRY

The changing history of Rogerstone from a small hamlet into a sprawling suburb of the city of Newport is illustrated in this fascinating collection of over 170 photographs, maps and drawings. *Rogerstone* documents the past of this community, from its industrial heritage – including the steelworks of Guest Keen and Nettlefolds, and the marshalling yard of the Great Western Railway – through to the sporting activities for which Rogerstone is well known.

0 7524 3506 X

The Tempus History of Wales
PRYS MORGAN

Wales was at the heart of the Industrial Revolution, with towns like Merthyr Tydfil driving the engine of the British Empire. The cultural and social divide between modern, industrialised Wales and the traditional agricultural areas is explored within this comprehensive volume.

0 7524 1983 8

If you are interested in purchasing other books published by Tempus, or in case you have difficulty finding any Tempus books in your local bookshop, you can also place orders directly through our website

www.tempus-publishing.com